The Renaissance in Europe

LYNNE ELLIOTT

 Crabtree Publishing Company

www.crabtreebooks.com

Author: Lynne Elliott
Editor-in-Chief: Lionel Bender
Editors: Lynn Peppas, Simon Adams
Proofreader: Crystal Sikkens
Project coordinator: Robert Walker
Photo research: Susannah Jayes
Design concept: Robert MacGregor
Designer: Malcolm Smythe
Production coordinator: Margaret Amy Salter
Production: Kim Richardson
Prepress technician: Margaret Amy Salter

With thanks to First Folio.

Cover photo: Marie de Medici, painted by Italian portraitist Alessandro Allori between 1590-1605.

Photo on page 1: Painting on the walls and ceiling of the Sistine Chapel in the Vatican, by Michelangelo.

This book was produced for Crabtree Publishing Company by Bender Richardson White.

Photographs and reproductions:

The Art Archive: Galleria d'Arte Moderna, Rome/Gianni Dagli Orti: page 5; Museo del Prado, Madrid/Gianni Dagli Orti: page 9; Bibliothèque Nationale, Paris: pages 15, 16; Museo Historico Nacional, Buenos Aires, Gianni Dagli Orti: page 18; Tate Gallery, London: page 20; Culver Pictures: page 21; Nationalmuseet Copenhagen, Denmark/Alfredo Dagli Orti: page 22; Farnese Palace, Caprarola/Alfredo Dagli Orti: page 23; Musée du Château de Versailles/Gianni Dagli Orti: page 31

The Bridgeman Art Library: Museo de Firenze Com'era, Florence, Italy/Alinari: page 4; Hamburger Kunsthalle, Hamburg, Germany: page 26; British Library, London, UK/British Library Board. All rights reserved: page 30

Corbis: © The Gallery Collection: cover; Gustavo Tomsich: page 14

The Granger Collection: pages 6, 25

iStockphoto.com: page 29

Topfoto: pages 1, 10, 12, 19, 28; Alinari: pages 8, 13; Roger-Viollet: pages 7, 11, 17, 27; The British Library/HIP: page 24

Library and Archives Canada Cataloguing in Publication

Elliott, Lynne, 1968-
  The Renaissance in Europe / Lynne Elliott.

(Renaissance world)
Includes index.
ISBN 978-0-7787-4591-4 (bound).--ISBN 978-0-7787-4611-9 (pbk.)

  1. Renaissance--Juvenile literature. 2. Europe--Civilization--Juvenile literature. I. Title. II. Series: Renaissance world (St. Catharines, Ont.)

CB361.E45 2009   j940.2   C2008-907902-7

Library of Congress Cataloging-in-Publication Data

Elliott, Lynne, 1968-
  The Renaissance in Europe / Lynne Elliott.
    p. cm. -- (Renaissance world)
  Includes index.
  ISBN 978-0-7787-4611-9 (pbk. : alk. paper) - -ISBN 978-0-7787-4591-4 (reinforced library binding : alk. paper)
  1. Renaissance--Juvenile literature. 2. Europe--Civilization--Juvenile literature. I. Title. II. Series.

CB361.E49 2009
940.2--dc22

2008052410

Crabtree Publishing Company

www.crabtreebooks.com   1-800-387-7650

Published in Canada
Crabtree Publishing
616 Welland Ave.
St. Catharines, Ontario
L2M 5V6

Published in the United States
Crabtree Publishing
PMB16A
350 Fifth Ave., Suite 3308
New York, NY 10118

Published in the United Kingdom
Crabtree Publishing
White Cross Mills
High Town, Lancaster
LA1 4XS

Published in Australia
Crabtree Publishing
386 Mt. Alexander Rd.
Ascot Vale (Melbourne)
VIC 3032

Contents

A Time of Rebirth 4

Renaissance People 6

Family Life 8

Health and Beauty 10

Renaissance Cities 12

Warfare 14

Trade and Banking 16

Exploration 18

Trade and Colonization 20

Religion 22

Science 24

Art and Society 26

The Visual Arts 28

Literature and Theater 30

Further Reading, Websites, Glossary, Index 32

A Time of Rebirth

The Renaissance was a time of great creativity in art, architecture, science, and literature. During this period, which lasted from about 1300 to 1600, important inventions such as the printing press and the telescope were made. Explorers ventured across the globe, beautiful buildings were constructed, and literature and theater also flourished at this time.

The Beginnings of the Renaissance

"Renaissance" means "rebirth" in French. The Renaissance began around 1300 in Italy, where statues, buildings, and works of art from the Roman Empire survived. Artists and writers in Italy thought the Roman, and the earlier ancient Greek civilizations, had reached the heights of achievement in art, architecture, literature, government, law, and **philosophy**. They began studying these areas of classical learning, now known as the humanities. They searched in the libraries of **monasteries** for handwritten copies of ancient books and also uncovered the remains of ancient buildings. Humanists, or those studying the humanities, hoped to use what they learned to improve their own society. They believed that, through their work, the glorious age of the Greek and Roman civilizations would be reborn.

The Renaissance began in Italian cities such as Florence. Humanist scholars living there among other writers, artists, and architects, as well as among prosperous businesspeople, used their wealth to buy paintings and sculptures to support artists.

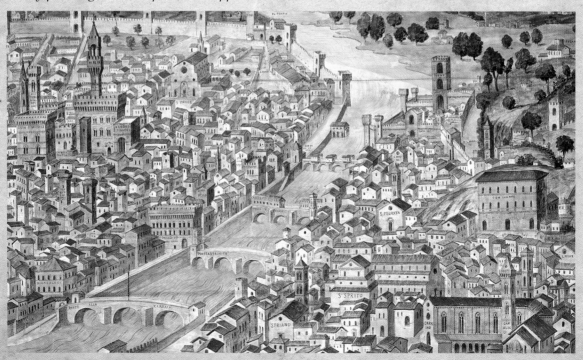

The Spread of the Renaissance

By the 1400s, the Renaissance was spreading northward throughout the rest of Europe. Artists returning from their studies in Italy, as well as travelers and merchants who had spent time in Italy, carried these new ideas home with them. The ideas of ancient scholars and humanists spread throughout Europe after German goldsmith Johannes Gutenberg developed the printing press in the 1450s. Before the printing press, copies of books and maps were made by hand, which was slow and costly. The printing press printed multiple copies of a book quickly and with far less cost than hand copying. Printers copied humanists' books, as well as Greek and Roman classics, and sold them to scholars throughout Europe.

To print a page, a printer put metal letters in a frame and then inked them. He put the frame on the press. By turning a huge wooden screw on the press, he brought down a block of wood that pressed a sheet of paper against the letters. The press made printing so easy that within 50 years of the invention of Gutenberg's press, between eight and ten million books had been printed by more than 1,000 printers throughout Europe.

TIMELINE

1290s: Giotto begins to change the nature of art by painting realistic people

1310s: Dante begins writing the *Divine Comedy,* considered the first great work of Renaissance literature

1450s: Gunpowder becomes more effective, and cannons are increasingly used in warfare

1455: The first European book, a copy of the Bible, is printed by Johannes Gutenberg

1492: Christopher Columbus sails to the Americas

1495-98: Leonardo da Vinci paints *The Last Supper*

1517: Martin Luther's list of grievances leads to the Protestant **Reformation**

1543: Andreas Vesalius dissects and draws diagrams of the human body

1547: Michelangelo designs St. Peter's Basilica in Rome, Italy

1599: William Shakespeare writes *Romeo and Juliet*

1609–10: Galileo Galilei uses the telescope to prove that the Sun is the center of the solar system

Renaissance People

During the Renaissance, most Europeans lived in the countryside, but many people began to move to cities and towns. They hoped to practice a trade in town workshops, study in city schools, or work as servants in townhouses. Cities soon became very crowded.

Peasants

Peasant men and women spent their lives growing crops and raising animals, from which they produced food and clothing for their families, for nobles, called lords, and for sale in nearby towns. Peasants lived and worked on the lord's estate, which included the lord's house or villa, peasant huts, stables, fields, orchards, vineyards, fishponds, and pastures.

Some peasants, called serfs, were given land to farm, but had to farm the lord's land a few days each month and were never allowed to leave the estate. Other peasants, called free peasants, rented land from the lord, did not have to work in the lord's fields, and could leave the estate if they wanted. All peasants paid taxes and fines to the lord in cash or in produce from the land.

Most peasants lived in small one- or two-room houses attached to the pen where they kept their animals, such as a cow, some pigs, chickens, goats, or sheep.

Town and City Dwellers

Artists, scholars, writers, church officials, craftspeople, tradespeople, and wealthy businesspeople all lived in cities. The most powerful city dwellers were the wealthy bankers and merchants. Bankers lent money to people for a profit. Merchants bought and sold goods such as fur and wool from northern Europe, spices from Asia, and gold and ivory from Africa. They used their wealth to build large homes, dress in splendid fabrics and jewelry, and **commission** works of art and literature. They also commissioned public buildings, such as churches and libraries.

Craftspeople made goods such as clothing and shoes, furniture, cooking pots, jewelry, mirrors, and glassware. Others worked with food. Butchers sold meat, bakers made bread and cakes, and spice grocers sold spices, oils, sugar, and honey. Each craft or trade had its own association called a guild. Guilds fixed the prices of goods and set standards for workmanship, wages, and the training of young craftspeople. Guilds were also social clubs that sponsored parades, plays, and the building of churches and chapels. In some European towns and cities, guild members also ran the local government.

*Nobles and courtiers dressed in expensive fabrics such as silk and **brocades**. Men wore floor-length **tunics** or short, fitted jackets known as doublets that were covered by capes. Women wore long dresses covered by capes or coats that were often lined with fur.*

Nobles and Courtiers

Nobles, men and women from powerful, wealthy families, ruled most of Europe during the Renaissance. The most powerful nobles were kings and queens, who ruled over vast areas of land called kingdoms. Kings and queens governed less important nobles, such as princes, dukes, or counts, who ruled smaller areas of land. An important noble had a court, or an assembly of advisors, called courtiers. These included family, friends, and government officials who advised rulers about government, lawmaking, **diplomacy**, and war.

Nobles and courtiers lived together in magnificent palaces with beautiful gardens, fishponds, and groves of trees. Court life was full of lavish ceremonies, including great feasts and **jousting** tournaments, which showed off the importance of the ruler.

Family Life

A typical Renaissance household included parents, children, and possibly grandparents. Wealthy families often had more than four children, sometimes ten or more, because they could afford to raise them. Most poorer families had no more than three children. Not many of these children could expect to survive into adulthood.

Birth and Infancy

The birth of a child during the Renaissance was a time of much joy and celebration, but also one of great danger. More than one in ten mothers died in childbirth and many babies died quickly from infection or from unsanitary conditions. Children were not born in hospitals but at home in their mothers' beds. They were usually delivered by female family members who were familiar with childbirth or occasionally by a midwife, a woman trained to deliver babies. Soon after the birth, babies were cleaned and then swaddled, or wrapped tightly in blankets, to keep them warm. They slept in their mothers' beds, or beside their mothers' beds in wooden cradles.

Childhood and Adolescence

Fewer than half of Renaissance children lived to adulthood. Malnutrition, infection, and diseases such as influenza, tuberculosis, and plagues took their lives. Those who survived the first few years of life spent their days with their mothers, playing with balls, sticks, puppets, and other homemade toys. As they grew older, children of peasants and townspeople helped their mothers with simple chores around the house or garden and enjoyed games such as marbles, hide and seek, and hopscotch.

Most mothers breastfed their babies, but wealthy families hired a wet nurse, a woman who fed the baby with her own milk. Babies breastfed until they could eat solid foods.

Growing Up

Older children were given more difficult chores to prepare them for adulthood. In the countryside, peasant girls were expected to know how to milk cows and care for the rest of the livestock. Peasant boys learned to farm and repair farming tools by helping their fathers. Peasant children did not usually learn to read and write. Children in towns learned a trade by helping in their parents' workshops. Some boys went to school to learn how to read and do enough arithmetic to run a business. Girls were not as likely to go to school or learn how to read, but they did learn important housekeeping skills at home from their mothers.

Wealthy townspeople and noble parents wanted their boys and girls to have a good education. They hired tutors who taught the children how to read and write in their native language and sometimes in **Latin**. In Italy, boys and girls went to city schools, where they learned how to read and write. Out of school, wealthy boys learned how to hunt and ride horses, while girls learned how to embroider, paint, and play music.

Renaissance couples exchanged marriage vows and wedding rings in front of a priest and wedding guests, who would join them for a feast after the ceremony. A bride received a gift, called a dowry, from her family. The dowry was usually money, furniture, clothing, and, in rare cases, land. It helped the new couple to set up their own household.

Marriage

Parents often arranged marriages for their children. Noble families used marriages to make political alliances, while merchant families used them to form business partnerships. Men were usually in their 20s or 30s when they got married. They worked outside the house, farming, working at their craft or in their business, or working in government. Women usually married between the ages of 14 and 20. A woman's main job was to bear and raise children and look after her husband. Peasant women worked in the home and the garden, cooking, cleaning, growing food, and raising farm animals. Craftswomen helped in their husbands' shops, while noblewomen governed their households and agricultural estates.

Health and Beauty

People in the Renaissance suffered from many diseases, some of which were dangerous or life-threatening. They got stomach viruses and food poisoning from spoiled food and dirty water. They lived with skin diseases caused by lice, fleas, and bedbugs in their clothing, hair, and linens. Infectious deadly diseases, such as the plague, smallpox, influenza, tuberculosis, and measles, spread rapidly, especially in crowded cities.

Doctors and Surgeons

Doctors in the Renaissance diagnosed illnesses by taking a patient's pulse and examining the color and clarity of body fluids, such as urine and blood. For treatment, doctors recommended changes in diet, exercise, such as hunting or dancing, and better personal hygiene. They prescribed bloodletting, which caused a person to bleed slightly by cutting them or applying bloodsucking leeches to their skin. Doctors believed that bloodletting restored the body's fluids, called humors, to a healthy balance by releasing extra humor.

Trepanning was a medical procedure that drilled a hole through a person's skull bone. Doctors performed it to relieve pressure in the brain and believed that it cured everything from headaches to mental illness. It was performed without any anesthesia.

Surgeons repaired bones and stitched up wounds, pulled teeth, and performed bloodletting. If necessary, they removed tumors, hernias, and kidney stones. They tried to avoid dangerous surgeries because people often died during surgery or afterward from infections.

Renaissance mothers provided home remedies for most of their family's illnesses. They made medicines from plants and herbs grown in home gardens and mixed them according to recipes found in books. If they were wealthy, families could afford to be treated by a university-trained doctor, who charged expensive fees for a home visit. Those who could not afford a doctor could seek treatment from the less expensive barber-surgeon or **apothecary**.

Beauty and Cosmetics

High foreheads on women were considered beautiful during the Renaissance. Women plucked or removed their forehead hair by rubbing it with a rough stone or burning it off with a chemical called quicklime. They also removed most of their eyebrows. Since pale complexions were fashionable, women applied white flour, chalk, or a harmful white lead powder mixed with water or olive oil to their faces. They then covered their faces with a thin glaze of egg white so that their makeup stayed on longer. Blond or light-red hair was also fashionable, so women lightened their hair with bleaches made from plants, eggs, and white wine. They also bleached it in the Sun by wearing hats that shaded their faces but allowed them to pull their hair through a hole in the top.

Renaissance men were also concerned about their appearances. They took time to groom their beards and mustaches and cut their hair just above their shoulders.

Wealthy Renaissance women grew their hair long and pulled it up into a lavish hairstyle ornately decorated with jewelry.

Hygiene

During the Renaissance, people took baths once a month or sometimes only once every three months. The wealthy bathed in indoor or outdoor tubs that servants filled with water heated by fire. Others bathed in rivers, streams, or in wooden tubs filled with cold water. People used soap and shampoos that were made from lye, which is a mixture of wood ash and water, and were scented with rose, lavender, or cypress. They applied hair and skin lotions made from milk, lard, or oils, which they perfumed with various spices. They also attached deodorant bags, called pomanders, which contained amber and apples, nutmeg, rosewater, and other herbs, to their belts.

Renaissance Cities

Renaissance cities grew in size and number. Most cities were located on major waterways and were centers of trade. Venice in Italy and Antwerp in Belgium were two of Europe's largest trading cities, with more than 100,000 people in each. Medium-sized cities, such as Florence and Rome in Italy, had about 60,000 people each. Most European cities were smaller, with up to 40,000 people.

Life in the City

At the beginning of the Renaissance, cities were often crowded, noisy, and smelly. Narrow, crooked, and unpaved streets were lined with shops selling everything from food and clothing to spices and medicines. Above these shops were tall, narrow townhouses that leaned out over the streets, blocking sunlight. Waste was often thrown into the streets or into streams and rivers.

Civic pride among leading Renaissance city dwellers inspired them to use their wealth to make their cities more beautiful. Wealthy families hired talented architects to build palaces and sometimes churches, while city governments commissioned them to build town halls and create large public squares. Painters and sculptors were hired to create artwork for these places. Streets were widened and wooden bridges were rebuilt in stone and decorated with statues.

The leader of the city of Venice was called the Doge. He was elected for life by the city's rich nobles.

Ruling the Cities

City governments passed laws, repaired city walls and roads, maintained courts and jails, controlled markets, and raised armies. Cities had many different kinds of government. Some were run directly by lords. Others, especially those in northern Europe, were free cities whose merchants and guild members had paid their lords for the right to govern themselves. These cities were run by officials elected by the citizens. Citizenship was limited to nobles and to merchants who were members of city guilds. Townspeople who were not guild members and peasants in the countryside were excluded.

The Republics

Some Italian cities were **republics**. In Venice, nobles elected the city's officials, while guild members elected the city council in Florence. Over time, wealthy families, such as the Medici banking family in Florence, gained power over the city councils and ruled the cities themselves.

Italian cities often had large squares, called piazzas, surrounded by important buildings, where the public gathered to watch parades, tournaments, and processions.

City-States

As trade, manufacturing, and banking increased, Italian trading cities became more important. Some cities became so powerful that they began to rule nearby smaller cities and towns and the people in the surrounding countryside. These territories were called city-states. Nobles ran some city-states, such as Milan, while city councils and leading families ran others, such as Venice and Florence.

Warfare

Renaissance city-states and their ruling families fought with one another for land and political power. If one city-state became too powerful, others would join forces and fight against that city-state to stop it from expanding. The nature of warfare changed greatly during this time.

The Knight and the Mercenary

In the **Middle Ages**, noblemen, called knights, were required to fight and provide an army of soldiers for their lords. By the Renaissance, knights and their lords had different arrangements. Many knights were still dedicated to the ideal of knighthood and to fighting but others preferred to stay home and manage their estates. These knights gave their lords money to hire professional soldiers to fight in their place.

The lords began to hire professional soldiers, called mercenaries, to defend their territories and pay them for their military service. These military commanders, in turn, hired and paid men from the impoverished lower classes to fight with them. In Italy, these commanders and their men were called *condottieri*. Unlike knights who were loyal to their lords and fought for honor and glory, *condottieri* were loyal to no one but the person or group of people who gave them the most money or land. Consequently, war turned into a substantial money-making enterprise.

Renaissance knights and mercenaries fought on horseback with lances, or long poles, that they used to knock their enemies off their horses. Foot soldiers marched into battle with pole-axes, long sticks with metal spikes at the tip that pierced the enemy's armor.

Fight and Force Pays

When mercenaries were not fighting, they did not earn any income, so some mercenaries prolonged feuds. In time of peace, although it was not widespread, some mercenaries stole money from unarmed travelers and threatened townspeople with harm until they gave the soldiers money to be left alone.

Siege Warfare

Warfare normally took place on battlefields, but during the Renaissance, cities came under increasing threat from siege warfare. A siege is an attack on a city from outside its walls, combined with a **blockade** of supplies coming into, and going out of, the city. The goal of a siege was to force the city to surrender due to a lack of food, water, weapons, or ammunition. Siege weapons included the trebuchet, a catapult that could throw 300-pound (136-kg) projectiles against or over city walls. Siege towers were wooden towers on wheels that could be pushed against city walls to allow soldiers to climb over the walls and into the city.

New Weapons

Renaissance soldiers fought with swords, bows and arrows, pikes or long poles with sharp spikes at the end, and crossbows. By the 1400s, more powerful weapons, called firearms, were developed. Firearms, such as guns and cannons, used the explosion of gunpowder to hurl objects, such as metal balls, long distances. The balls from an arquebus, or gun, could pierce a soldier's armor, while flying cannonballs could crush city walls and defenses, making cannons a favorite siege weapon. Cannons were also mounted on city walls to defend against attackers and attached to decks of ships to fire cannonballs against an enemy fleet.

While laying siege to a city or castle, Renaissance military leaders combined traditional weapons, such as bows to shoot arrows at enemy soldiers, with newly invented cannons to destroy the walls of cities or castles.

Trade and Banking

During the Renaissance, making and trading goods became two important ways to earn money. Banking arose from trade and from merchants' need to store, borrow, and send money to run their businesses. As trade grew, banking became more complex.

Trade

Renaissance merchants traded a wide variety of goods across Europe, Asia, and Africa. Many of these items came from the natural resources, or raw materials, of an area. Northern Europe produced wood, amber, wool, fur, and fish. Southern Europe had silk, linen, and wool, as well as grapes to make wine. From even farther away came Middle Eastern citrus fruits, Indonesian spices, Egyptian cotton, and Indian jewels. In addition to these raw materials, merchants traded manufactured goods. They sold Florentine woolen cloth, Chinese silk, Flemish tapestries, and Venetian glass and mirrors, as well as books and weapons.

To transport goods from the East to Europe, traders used the Silk Road. Horse and camel caravans, as well as ships, carried goods along this ancient trading route, which ran for thousands of miles from Asia through the Middle East to the Mediterranean Sea and Europe. The Silk Road was important to Renaissance Europe until Portuguese sailors in the late 1400s found a sea route to India and brought goods back on their own ships.

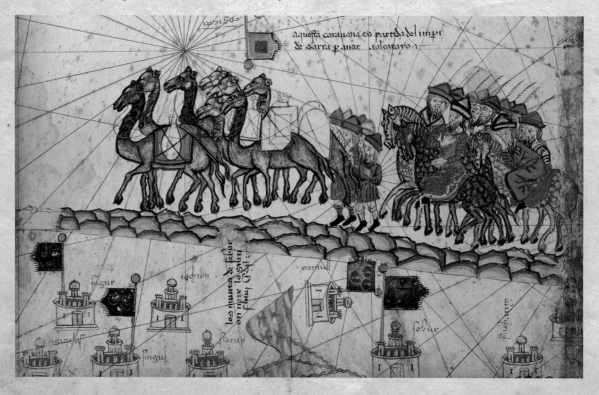

Markets and Fairs

Local trade was usually conducted at tradespeople's shops or at markets in city and town squares, where vendors set up stalls or carts displaying their goods. People from the city and nearby countryside came to marketplaces to buy food, clothing, cloth, cosmetics, and household items, such as cookware. Long-distance trade took place at fairs, which were large international markets held a few times a year, usually near important cities and towns throughout Europe. As international trade grew, fairs became less important because merchants set up permanent trading businesses in Europe's main coastal and riverfront cities. There they shipped, received, bought, displayed, sold, and stored goods from all over the world.

Money and Banking

During the Renaissance, city-states and the rulers of other states minted, or made, their own gold and silver coins. There were hundreds of different types of coins in circulation. Moneychangers, usually merchants who knew the value of European coins, exchanged different currencies so that people from different parts of Europe could do business with one another.

Merchant moneychangers gradually became merchant-bankers during the Renaissance. They were located in cities and towns, where tradespeople and other merchants did business. People gave merchant-bankers their money for safekeeping and borrowed money from them. Merchant-bankers also created "bills of exchange," an early type of check that could be sent to a merchant in another city to buy goods. For each transaction, the merchant-bankers charged a fee and became very wealthy.

Moneychangers worked in marketplaces and in city offices where they were surrounded by the tools of their trade, such as gold coins and scales. Scales measured a coin's weight, which told the moneychanger if anyone had tampered with its value by shaving or filing gold off it.

Exploration

During the Middle Ages, Arab and Turkish merchants and governments controlled Europe's trade with the Indies, that is India, China, and the Spice Islands in what is now Indonesia. Renaissance rulers and merchants wanted to end Arab and Turkish control over trade and avoid paying their high tolls and taxes on Asian goods. To do this, they needed to find a sea route to the East and trade directly with merchants there. During the 1500s, most major European countries were competing to find this route. Later, they set up colonies in these lands.

The Search for the Indies

Portuguese explorers were the first European adventurers to reach India by sea. In 1497, Vasco da Gama sailed around the southernmost tip of Africa, up the East African coastline, and across the sea to India. In addition to setting up trading posts along the way, he brought back much valuable information for mapmakers to chart the course to the East. This information was kept secret by the Portuguese government in order to keep competitors out of the area. Portugal soon became very wealthy from its eastern trade.

Columbus's fleet of three ships included the Nina *and the* Pinta, *two small, fast ships called caravels, and the* Santa Maria, *a bulkier cargo ship called a carrack.*

Discovering America

While Portuguese ships sailed eastward to reach the Indies, Christopher Columbus, an explorer sponsored by the Spanish king and queen, believed he could get there by sailing west. No one knew at the time that a large landmass, now called North and South America, lay between Europe and Asia.

In 1492, Columbus prepared his fleet of three ships for a voyage into the unknown. He found a crew and loaded the ships with provisions, including food, water, weapons, and goods to trade, such as bells and glass beads. The fleet sailed for two months across the Atlantic Ocean before sighting land. Columbus believed that he had finally reached Asia, but, in truth, he had landed in the Bahamas. Spain claimed these and the surrounding islands as its own territories.

Conquistadors

Other Spanish explorers, known as conquistadors, set out from the Caribbean islands to claim new lands and gold for Spain. In 1521, Hernán Cortés conquered Montezuma's Aztec empire after laying siege to the capital city of Tenochtitlán, now Mexico City. Conquistador Francisco Pizarro led an expedition to South America and took over the Inca empire for himself and Spain. The Spanish conquistadors treated the native peoples brutally. They killed, tortured, or forced them to work as slaves, growing crops, transporting goods, and mining silver, copper, and gold. The conquistadors also brought horses to the Americas. Since the native peoples had never seen such animals before, they were terrified by them.

During the siege of Tenochtitlán, the Spanish cut off supplies, including food and water, to the city. The Aztecs surrendered after three months, weakened by starvation and disease.

Trade and Colonization

Since Spanish explorers dominated Central and South America, the English, French, and Dutch explorers concentrated on North America. They tried to find a sea route to India by going over the top of or through North America. This route, which was not successfully navigated until the early 1900s, is called the Northwest Passage. While searching for this passage, French explorer Jacques Cartier discovered the St. Lawrence Gulf and River. Martin Frobisher, from England, sailed past Greenland to the far northeastern corner of Canada. English explorer Henry Hudson's exploration took him up and down the eastern coasts of America and Canada.

New World Products

The main goal of many explorers was to bring back gold and silver from the Americas, called the "New World" by Europeans as opposed to the Old World of Europe. They also brought back new things that Europeans had never seen before, such as sweet potatoes, maize, cocoa, pumpkins, squash, vanilla, tomatoes, coconuts, and pineapples. To the New World, Europeans brought wheat, grapes, olives, lemons, oranges, rice, bananas, and sugar crops. They brought animals such as horses, pigs, cattle, and chickens. They also brought European diseases, such as smallpox, influenza, and measles, which devastated the native populations, who had no natural resistance.

During his last voyage, in 1611, Henry Hudson's crew mutinied, or rebelled, against him. They set him, his son, and seven loyal crew members adrift in an open boat without food or water in the icy bay that now bears his name: Hudson's Bay. He was never seen again.

Settlement and Colonization

After the explorers mapped out the Americas, Europeans set up colonies there. Colonies were territories that had strong ties to their founder countries back in Europe. The Spanish settled in Mexico and Central and South America; the English founded settlements in Virginia and New England; the French settled in Canada; the Dutch settled around New York; and the Portuguese settled in South America. Many, but not all, native peoples tolerated the earliest European settlers. Some even helped the Europeans survive starvation and bad weather. As more and more Europeans settled, native peoples were pushed off their lands or died due to European diseases.

The Northeast Passage

Between 1553 and 1597, the English explorers Sir Hugh Willoughby and Richard Chancellor and the Dutchman Willem Barents tried to find a route to the Indies by sailing round Scandinavia and Northern Russia. This was known as the Northeast Passage. They failed because the Arctic Sea is frozen for much of the year. Chancellor did reach the far north of Russia and from there trekked overland south to Moscow. He set up a European trading company dealing in silks, cottons, and wools from Russia, China, and Japan. The company lasted until 1917.

*The Europeans came to the Americas in search of gold and **conquest** and to convert the native peoples to Christianity. They also came to trade, offering manufactured goods such as tools and knife blades, in exchange for gold, furs, and other luxury items.*

Religion

Most people in Renaissance Europe were Christian. They believed in one God, and in the teachings of his son, Jesus Christ, whom they believed was the savior of humankind. Religion was an important part of people's daily lives.

The Roman Catholic Church

At the beginning of the Renaissance, all Christians in western Europe belonged to one church, the Roman Catholic Church, which was led by the pope. People tried to live their lives according to the teachings of the church, which meant worshiping God, attending church services, and receiving the sacraments, or rites, of the church. They celebrated holy days, such as Easter, and days dedicated to holy people, called saints. They also built chapels and churches.

The Reformation

The Reformation split European Christians into two groups, Catholic and Protestant. The Reformation began in 1517 when a **friar** named Martin Luther wrote a public challenge to some church teachings and nailed it to the door of a church in Wittenberg, Germany.

Luther challenged the church on many issues. He disliked the fact that the church was making money selling indulgences, documents that people could buy or earn with good deeds and which replaced doing penance or punishment for their sins. He also challenged the leadership of the pope and the **hierarchy** of churchmen, believing that people could direct their own religious education by reading the Bible. Luther translated the Bible from Latin, the language of scholars and churchmen, into German, the language of everyday people.

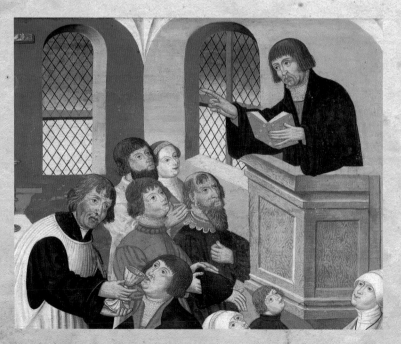

Followers of Martin Luther stripped their churches of Catholic symbols of faith, such as statutes, artwork, and tapestries depicting Mary, the mother of Jesus, and saints. These figures were not important to Lutheran beliefs.

The Catholic Counter-Reformation

The Reformation massively damaged the authority of the pope and of the Catholic Church. To **refute** Protestant teachings and to reform his own church, the pope called together more than 200 high-ranking church officials for an important series of meetings in Trent, Northern Italy, beginning in 1545. These meetings became known as the Council of Trent. The Council confirmed Catholic teachings, declared that the Latin Bible was the official and authorized version, and that religious instruction was the duty of churchmen only. It also reformed the sale of indulgences and enforced discipline in the church. It forbade churchmen to become wealthy and called for the better education of all priests.

The Protesters

Luther and others, including the Frenchman John Calvin, sparked a debate among Christians. Eventually, their followers broke away from the Roman Catholic Church and created their own churches. Although first known as "reformers," their followers later became known as "protestants" because they protested orders to halt the Reformation.

The Council of Trent was actually three different meetings that spanned 18 years and were led by three consecutive popes. It was considered one of the most important councils in the history of the Catholic Church.

Science

While earlier scholars had relied on religious teachings and on the writings of scientific authorities from the past, Renaissance scientists began to observe nature and study it firsthand. These new ways of learning marked the start of an age called the "Scientific Revolution," which extended into the 1800s.

Astronomy

Before the Renaissance, astronomers believed the ancient theory that Earth was the center of the solar system and that it stayed still while the Sun, the other planets, and the stars revolved around it. Renaissance astronomers proved that this old theory was wrong. Nicholas Copernicus, a Polish astronomer, mathematically calculated that Earth was always moving and that it revolved around the Sun once a year. In 1543, he published his radical theory in a book called *On the Revolutions of the Celestial Spheres.*

Copernicus's work showed that Earth had a daily rotation on its own axis and a yearly rotation around the Sun.

The Theory is Proved

Only a handful of scientists believed Copernicus's theory, until an Italian mathematician and astronomer named Galileo Galilei helped prove him right. In 1609, Galileo developed a telescope with which he could observe the Sun and the planets, especially Jupiter, to prove that Earth and the other planets were spinning while rotating around the Sun. People were suspicious of scientists who disagreed with ancient teachings. Martin Luther criticized Copernicus, while the Catholic Church eventually forced Galileo to renounce or give up his views.

Chemistry and Alchemy

Some scientists who worked with chemicals in the Renaissance were known as alchemists. Early alchemists were interested in changing less valuable metals, such as lead, into gold or finding a potion that would cure all illnesses. They failed, but their work in classifying and comparing different substances and how they reacted with one another led to the modern science of chemistry.

Anatomy

Before the Renaissance, doctors' knowledge of health and the body was based on ancient texts filled with many incorrect theories. Medieval scientists were not allowed to dissect human corpses to find out how the body really worked because the church believed that dissection took away the dignity of the deceased person. A great advance in **anatomy** came in 1543, when Andreas, Vesalius, a Flemish doctor, began dissecting and studying human bodies, usually those of executed criminals. He wrote a book, based on his findings, about the structure of the human body and how its organs, muscles, and bones worked. Doctors gradually rejected the old theories and began to observe patients directly, gathering more accurate information on how the body was made up and how it functioned.

Vesalius is sometimes referred to as the "father of anatomy" because he was the first scientist to dissect, describe, and detail the human body in drawings.

Art and Society

The Renaissance is best known for its many artistic achievements. Great artists created beautiful paintings, sculptures, and buildings. Most of this activity began in Italy but it soon spread to influence art and culture in the great cities and towns of northern Europe.

Altarpieces were religious pictures that were placed behind or on the altar of a Christian church to inspire religious devotion in those who saw it. They were often divided into several sections and framed individually.

New Subjects

Renaissance artists, like the medieval artists that came before them, portrayed religious subjects in their work but they differed from earlier artists because they began to depict many non-religious scenes as well. They sculpted ancient gods from Greek and Roman mythology and painted scenes from history such as famous battles. They chose landscapes and wildlife as subjects of their paintings. Renaissance artists also painted and sculpted the human body and portraits of individuals and their families.

Renaissance artists sometimes incorporated the faces of patrons and their families into their artwork. Sandro Botticelli painted the faces of some of the Medici family on the figures in his Adoration of the Magi. His own face might appear on the figure in the lower right-hand corner of the picture.

Renaissance master artists were usually skilled at working with more than one type of material, or medium. Some, like Michelangelo, were great painters, sculptors, and even architects. Renaissance artists also designed medals, furniture, tombs, costumes, decorations for festivals, and illustrations for books. Leonardo da Vinci represented the Renaissance ideal of a "universal man," a person who was accomplished in many different fields. He was a famed painter and architect, who also wrote works on anatomy, mathematics, and astronomy. He designed early kinds of calculators, parachutes, robots, airplanes, and war machines such as tanks. He drew and recorded his many ideas in a series of notebooks.

The Artist as a Professional

Medieval artists were humble craftspeople. During the Renaissance, the status of some artists rose to that of a professional. The public took an interest in art and a pride in skilled local artists. Such artists gained the respect of learned people, rulers, and church leaders. They were seen as talented geniuses. Renaissance artists began to sign their work in order to be recognized. When they became famous, they were paid well for their art.

Patrons

To earn an income, artists hoped to be hired by wealthy people and institutions known as patrons. The Catholic Church was the richest patron of Renaissance artists, architects, glassmakers, sculptors, and embroiderers, who made altar cloths with religious scenes on them. Wealthy families also commissioned and bought art, often portraits of themselves or their families. Some patrons established academies, or schools, to encourage scholarship and the arts. Michelangelo studied in one of the studios set up in the Medici household to encourage talented young artists.

The Visual Arts

A New Approach

In the Middle Ages, artists painted people as if they were stiff and flat. Renaissance artists painted their subjects in a more realistic way. They gave their subjects lifelike facial expressions and natural poses, and used shadows to create a sense of depth. The painter credited with first developing such techniques was Giotto di Bondone, who lived in Italy at the end of the 1200s. During the 1400s, painters began to experiment with perspective, a method of drawing something on a flat surface so that it appears to have three-dimensional depth, just as the eye would see it in real life.

Paints

Renaissance artists experimented with new ways of creating, mixing, and using paint. Medieval painters made paint from water mixed with pigments, which are colors obtained from such objects as ground clay, stones, insects, plants, or shells. Renaissance artists applied this watercolor paint to fresh, wet plaster to create works of art called frescoes on walls or ceilings. The wet plaster dried quickly with the paint in it. Artists also used a substance called tempera, which is a pigment mixed with a quick-drying egg yolk, to paint on surfaces such as wood, canvas, or dry plaster.

More than 20 years after painting the frescoes on the enormous ceiling of the Sistine Chapel in the Vatican in Rome, Michelangelo returned in 1536 to paint The Last Judgment *on the wall behind the altar. Some of his holy figures were naked, which was considered to be immoral and obscene, so later artists, such as Daniele da Volterra, were commissioned to cover up the figures.*

Oil Paint

Northern European artists, such as Jan and Hubert van Eyck, began to experiment with oils mixed with pigments. Oil paints dried slowly and gave artists more time to paint. Oils could also be painted on top of one another and blended to create different textures and shades of light and dark.

Architecture

Ancient Roman ruins surrounded Italian architects of the Renaissance. These men studied the ancient buildings and copied the designs. They borrowed the ideas of round columns, wide arches, spacious interiors, and large domes in their work. Architects also studied mathematics to make their buildings, bridges, and gardens symmetrical and proportional, with regular and balanced patterns.

Sculpture and Relief

Renaissance sculptors created large statues, monuments, and fountains. They carved furniture, small medals, and other decorative items for homes, palaces, churches, and other public buildings. They also carved reliefs, which were scenes sculpted out of a flat surface. Sculptors worked with bronze, wood, terracotta, marble, or limestone, and sometimes with more expensive materials such as gold, silver, and ivory. Although much of their work was religious, they also depicted figures from ancient myths and history, as well as patrons, nobles, and military heroes of their day.

Filippo Brunelleschi designed and built the dome of the cathedral in Florence after observing the dome of the ancient Pantheon in Rome. His dome was 138 feet (42 m) wide and 133 feet (40 m) high.

Literature and Theater

Literature and theater were two forms of Renaissance entertainment. Literature tells stories with the written word. Since most people in the Renaissance could not read, books were enjoyed by a small and privileged section of society. Theater tells stories with spoken words and could be enjoyed by everyone.

Translations and Imitations

Renaissance writers and poets were very interested in the writings of the ancient Romans and Greeks. They translated their histories, plays, **epics**, and poetry, and imitated the ideas and style of these classical books in their own works.

During the Renaissance, writers also began to write in the vernacular, or local native language. Geoffrey Chaucer of England wrote *The Canterbury Tales* in Middle English, the language used in England from around 1150 to 1500. The Italian writer Giovanni Boccaccio wrote his masterpiece, *The Decameron*, and several poems and romances in Italian.

In The Canterbury Tales, *a group of travelers journey to the shrine of St. Thomas à Becket in Canterbury, England. Along the way, each traveler tells a tale that highlights good and bad characteristics of people in 14th-century English society.*

Renaissance Libraries

In the Middle Ages, monasteries and universities kept books in their own libraries for the private use of monks, scholars, and students. In the Renaissance, rulers created both private and public libraries. Cosimo de' Medici opened the first public library in Florence in the 1440s. Other leaders in Italy and England followed his example. Although these libraries were public, they were places of study used by scholars and students who could read. Books were not borrowed from libraries. In fact, because they were still so expensive, books were chained to the shelves to prevent theft and damage.

Theater

Plays took place in noble households, city squares, and the courtyards of inns and taverns. During the 1500s, people built permanent theaters or playhouses, much like the Greeks and Romans had done. Theaters were usually outdoors, with layers of seating surrounding a raised stage. Plays were usually performed during fairs, festivals, and feast days. Many of these plays were religious in subject matter and taught moral lessons to the audience, but theater groups also began to perform Greek and Roman tragedies and comedies. Humanist scholars translated these classics into the vernacular languages of Renaissance Europe.

Renaissance writers also wrote their own plays for troupes of actors. England's most famous playwright and poet, William Shakespeare, wrote comedies, tragedies, historical plays, and romances for his theater troupe, the Lord Chamberlain's Men.

Women from all classes of English society could go to the theater to see one of Shakespeare's plays, but they could not perform in them. Female roles had to be performed by boys.

William Shakespeare was born in Stratford-upon-Avon in England in 1564 but spent most of his working life in theaters in the capital, London. He wrote 39 plays, as well as many poems. He died in Stratford in 1616.

Further Reading and Websites

Mason, Antony. *Everyday Life in Renaissance Times.* Minnesota: Smart Apple Media, 2006
Quigley, Mary. *The Renaissance.* Heinemann, 2003
Cole, Alison. *Eyewitness: Renaissance.* Dorling Kindersley, 2000
Morley, Jacqueline. *A Renaissance Town.* New York: Peter Bedrick, 2001
Shapiro, Stephen. *The Siege: Under Attack in Renaissance Europe.* Toronto: Annick Press, 2007

Teacher Oz's Kingdom of History—Renaissance www.teacheroz.com/renaissance.htm
Renaissance Connection www.renaissanceconnection.org
Exhibits Collection—Renaissance www.learner.org/interactives/renaissance
Elizabethan Era www.elizabethan-era.org.uk

Glossary

anatomy How the parts of a human, animal, or plant are arranged and work together

apothecary Someone who provides medicines or remedies

blockade Preventing supplies or people from entering or exiting a place

brocades Fabrics woven with a raised pattern

commission To hire someone to make or do something for you

conquest Something won in war or battle

diplomacy Settling issues, forming a relationship, between nations by treaties or agreements

epics Stories of a hero's adventures, usually written as a long poem

friar Male member of a Christian religious group

hierarchy An order of importance, ranking

jousting Sport where two knights try to knock each other off their horses using a lance, or long pole

Latin The language used in ancient Rome

Middle Ages Period of European history from about AD 400 to the Renaissance, also known as Medieval times

monasteries Places where monks or nuns lived to follow religious rules

or practices

philosophy Study of the rules or truths to be found about all areas of life or the universe

Reformation Religious movement to change the practices of the Roman Catholic Church resulting in the start of Protestant churches

refute To argue against something; prove false

republics Areas governed by an elected ruler, not one who inherited the position, such as a monarch

tunic A loose long shirt, often sleeveless, worn belted at the waist

Index

alchemy 25
anatomy 25, 27
art 4, 5, 7, 12, 26, 27, 28, 29
artists 4, 5, 7, 26, 27, 287, 29
astronomy 24, 27
bankers 7, 17
banking 13, 16, 17
beauty 11
children 8, 9, 19, 26, 31
cities 4, 6, 7, 9, 10, 12–13, 15, 17, 19, 26, 31
city-states 13, 14, 17
colonization 21
conquistadors 19
cosmetics 11
Counter-Reformation 23

courtiers 7
craftspeople 7, 9, 27
diseases 8, 10, 19, 20, 21
doctors 10, 25
explorers 18, 19, 20, 21
guilds 7, 12, 13
hygiene 11
knights 14
literature 4, 5, 7, 30
markets and fairs 17
marriage 9
mercenaries 14
merchants 5, 7, 9, 12, 16, 17, 18
money 17
nobles 6, 7, 9, 12, 13, 14, 29, 31

painting 12, 26, 27, 28, 29
patrons 27, 29
peasants 6, 8, 9, 12
printing 4, 5
Protestants 5, 22, 23
Reformation 5, 22, 23
religion 22, 23
Renaissance, definition of 4
Roman Catholic Church 22, 23, 24, 27
siege warfare 15
surgery 10
theater 4, 30, 31
trade 12, 13, 16, 17, 18, 19, 20, 21
warfare 14, 15

Printed in the U.S.A. — CG